Live for Them

Deborah Fullwood

Wild Ink Publishing LLC

Wild Ink Publishing

A Wild Ink Publishing Original
Wild Ink Publishing LLC
wild-ink-publishing.com

ISBN: (Paperback) 978-1-958531-14-3
ISBN: (eBook): 978-1-958531-15-0

To my beautiful family - my daughters Abbie and Layla and my husband Steve, I would not be the survivor I am today without their love and support.

Also, I'd like to acknowledge the nurses, doctors, specialists, surgeons, psychologists, and support people who work in the West Australian public health system - I owe my life to you.

Dear Reader,

On that morning, I woke and checked my email to find a submission. I almost filed it away, but something stopped me in my tracks, and begged me to read it immediately. This poet survived breast cancer. This poet needed, deserved, my full attention.

I knew the answer would be "yes" even before reading. Why? I knew it would be good. I was right. It's better than good, it's brilliant. How did I know it would be great? When artists create, and when poets write, we dig deep into our souls to find truth. Then we take that truth, twist it inside out, and face it head-on. We use our craft to look at our traumas and deal with them in the healthiest way possible, to create in a way that gives others hope. Hope being the key word here.

Deborah takes what she has gone through and turns it into poetic beauty. These poems are real and raw. She holds no punches. But she also stops from time to time to express how her love is abundant and to express the joy she receives from her family.

In *Live for Them*, Fullwood has creates a masterpiece of truth.

So, pour yourself a cup of tea, curl up under your favorite quilt, and take part in the depths of Fullwood's heart. You will come away a changed person.

With Love,
Abigail Wild
Wild Ink Publishing

Table of Contents

No Rules

I'll write until I feel myself let go.

My words like hair in the wind,

Strands dancing out of control

to the unstructured melody of mother nature's song.

No ties, no rules, just freedom

to become entwined with my thoughts.

Thoughts too deep for burden

but too strong to keep confined.

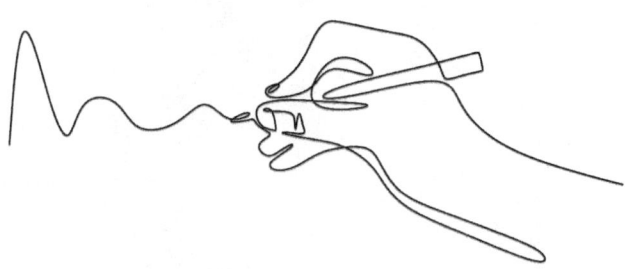

Warrior

A warrior still fights with
their scars.

Silhouette

In the darkness of life

be as bold as your silhouette;

unbreakable, consistent, and true

completely unaffected by the intricate details of existence

Live for Them

I was once invincible,

The world seemed calm and bright.

My chaos, self-inflicted,

Pain and sadness out of sight.

That world I knew came crashing down,

So suddenly in a day.

The words that no one wants to hear,

The words that make you pray.

But you're so young, the doctor said,

With tears in her eyes.

I buried my face, collapsed inside,

Shielding my family from my cries.

Not long after, I chose my path,

Decided to fight back stronger.

I had no choice but to live my life,

To live a little longer.

Live for Them

They watched me lose my hair in time,

They saw me frail and weak.

But every day they hugged me tight,

We love you they would speak.

My view of life has changed again,

They pulled me through the trench.

Survived my battle and kicked its ass,

We made it off the bench.

We're kicking goals and smashing dreams,

Together we are flying.

Cancer really pushed us round,

But we're no longer crying.

There will be days of grief and trauma,

The poison left a mark.

I'll dust it off and carry on,

My family needs my spark.

They need to know I'll live for them;

I'll do the best I can.

I'll be their light when things get dark,

When things don't go to plan.

A Moment

A moment in fear

will determine your

true strength.

Before

A week and a month,

days would go by

Living my life,

with barely a cry.

The sun came up

and the kids would play.

The day filled with laughter

"Be safe" I would pray.

Giving life to my children,

My heart, and my soul,

To feed them and hug them

Nothing else made me whole.

My husband would tell me,

each day, and each night.

He loved me so deeply

He'd hold me so tight.

Live for Them

It all seemed so normal,

so easy and kind.

It's so hard to think

I'd leave it behind.

All the things I had built

All the things I loved dear,

Are the things that I'll cherish

When my ending is near.

Battle

The difference is our battle.

The likeness is our ability to overcome anything with support.

Find a space to fight your own war,

surrounded by others who need your aid,

we will win together.

Flashbacks

A black and white blur

Sterile jelly smeared upon the confronting device

accompanied by a familiar feeling

- an emotional flashback.

The machine once revealing my baby's heartbeat,

a gentle flicker that filled my own heart with joy

was now, instead sealing my fate.

Progressively revealing the depth of my misfortune.

That joy is gone.

But now a new memory

of why I need to survive is formed

- an emotional flashback for the future.

Hope

I lay,

I breathe,

I wonder what will be,

I hurt,

I cry,

I pick myself up,

I carry on for them,

I smile, sweetly through clenched teeth.

I hope.

Surgery Day

The alarm would sound,

an early start.

Nerves would twitch,

right through my heart.

I'd paint a smile,

upon my face.

Cuddle the kids

and begin the race.

The doctors, nurses,

all hospital staff.

Arriving for work,

all having a laugh.

My husband was there,

every step of the way.

He'd kiss my head,

while I'm wheeled away.

Needles that poked

and prodded my skin.

I'd scrunch up my nose,

it was about to begin.

Eventually my eyes,

would heavily fall.

I'd drift off to sleep,

no worries at all.

I'd wake, not long later,

the questions all there.

Has the cancer all gone?

What's left? Am I bare?

The bandages strapped,

all over my chest.

They hide the new me,

it's all for the best.

Live for Them

Once I had strength,

we left straight away

Back to my children

with whom I would lay.

They looked at me weak,

and held my hand tight

Its ok now mummy,

you'll be alright.

The first big hurdle

was now over and done.

My body has changed,

but my body had won.

Guilt

The patient cries.

Not because of the pain or the scars,

Nor the thought of mortality,

But the guilt of knowing her family is helpless and hurting

because of her.

Pain

The hurt is like slices,

from knives cutting deep.

Of sand that whips sideways

From the wind as you weep.

It hurts like your toe

When the wall's in the way,

It bangs, and you scream

You drop down and you lay.

The pain is like hearing,

The chalk board with nails.

Of standing for hours

Without any rails.

Most of my pain

Was treated with meds,

But the pain that hurt most,

Was all in my head.

I couldn't escape

All the guilt in my mind

All the thoughts of my death

Leaving babies behind.

I wish that the pain

Was what everyone saw,

From the obvious cuts

all the wounds that were raw.

But it wasn't the case

All my pain was not there

The outside was cured

But the inside was bare.

Scarred

His touch feels foreign, a feeling of nothingness.

A twist of purple and white

Small rivers of trauma,

Flowing through the once, unmarked skin.

Fingertips navigating over the healed wound,

a rutted edge from a war of health,

no sensation or warmth.

A gentle caress sparks self-conscious conviction

but with it, a feeling of acceptance.

His touch feels foreign, but a feeling of love.

Steroids

Steroids made my body cope
With chemo every week.
As if the poisons weren't enough,
The steroids made me eat!

All the food, the tasty things,
The sugar, and the sweets,
Tasted terrible, tasted foul,
I needed some new treats!

Feeling hungry all the time,
There's never satisfaction.
The taste of metal on my tongue
Unfortunate reaction.

Be healthy, they would say to me,
Try to eat what's good.
But carbs were all my body craved,
I never understood.

Live for Them

The doctor didn't mind though,

He said that its ok.

We'll focus on survival now,

And weight another day.

Once the chemo finished,

The steroids to an end.

My taste buds back, ten kilos on,

The carbs were not my friend.

I did my best, went day by day

It truly was a struggle

I lost so much, but I'm alive,

And now there's more to snuggle!

Feeling

The hot water rolls over my body,

trying anything to relieve the pain.

Droplets feel like needles on my sensitive skin,

chemo trying to escape through my flesh.

A feeling of vulnerability.

The room fogs with steam, covering my reflections

so I do not have to see what's staring back at me.

A feeling of disrepair.

My scalp aches. The hairs forcefully evacuated from the inside;

each follicle squeezing tight and holding on in desperation.

A gentle touch feels like a hard knock.

A feeling of agony.

This is temporary, A process to survive.

A feeling of belief.

Emerge

A concoction of poison,

So strong and powerful.

Seeping through my veins like lava

Temporarily destroying innocence in its path.

When the poison dries up,

I will emerge from destruction,

And bloom, brighter and more radiant that ever before.

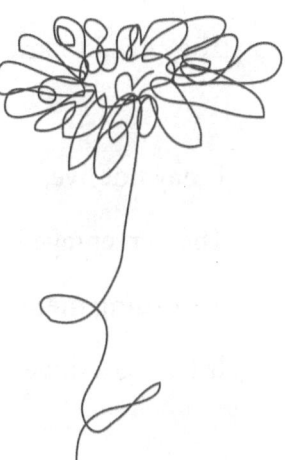

Photos

A thousand memories,

Passed in a blink,

The baby photos,

All dressed in pink.

Behind the lens

I use to hide,

The photos now,

I'm by their side.

The things we did,

Places we go,

Will remind my kids,

They need to know.

I may not live,

The percentage high,

Recording memories,

If I say goodbye.

Live for Them

I'll try my best;

I've told them so.

They'll hug these pics

If they're feeling low.

A thousand memories,

Passed in a blink.

If I leave this earth

they're our missing link.

Pink Ribbons

The pink ribbon.

A thin fabric of hope,

Of stranger's love,

Pinned in a twist,

A universal embrace.

Nurses

After the news,

the freight train shock.

The doctor then leaves,

My heart feels like rock.

A gentle voice speaks,

From behind the closed door.

Knock, knock she says softly,

Tears fall to the floor.

She walks in the room,

Her heart on her sleeve,

A presence so calming,

Please do not leave.

She kneels down beside me;

Her warm hands hold tight.

Explains all the jargon,

Makes sure I'm alright.

I say she and her,

that's more common than not.

But the male nurse staff,

I haven't forgot.

They are the ones there,

Through thick and through thin.

I can't thank them enough,

Where would I begin?

The doctors are special,

Their skills saved my life.

And without their hard work,

I'd be in some strife.

But often I think,

All the time nurses cared.

The ones that I turned to,

When I was so scared.

My Light

Because of your spark

I could ignite myself,

I could light up my path,

And illuminate survival

Change

My babies, don't cry

Just know that I'll fight for you like a lioness for her cubs.

My hair will fall, replaced with silk scarves -

all the beautiful colours of the rainbow.

My chest, remodeled like Barbie - nipple-less and unbreakable.

My body will change, but I will be stronger.

I will be me, and you will be you.

I will love you both, forever.

Exterior Perception

Our exterior is a weird state,

forever changing looks.

Relying on other opinions,

The kind, the hard, the books.

I used to care a lot about,

The way I was portrayed.

Until one day it dawned on me,

I shouldn't be afraid.

My life was flipped and faced with death;

It didn't matter anymore.

My hair, my face, my body sick,

Lucky I had my core.

The strangers stare, the sorry smiles,

The giveaway was the scarf.

I smiled back and made them see,

That I will always laugh.

The outside of me wilted,

My head completely bare.

My brows and lashes gone but one,

One remaining little hair.

I've learned since then, what matters most,

Is not what you can see,

But what's inside of someone's soul,

That matters most to me.

I now have hair, curls, and greys,

My brows, and lashes back.

Beanies packed, scarves are folded,

Neatly in a stack.

Appreciate your health,

And your happiness as well.

There will always be the cruel ones,

ignore and you'll excel.

Your exterior is a gorgeous thing,

A cover of your book.

Life is short, don't waste your time,

Embrace your unique look.

Body Image

A body that once was,

Has changed for the better;

cold, nipple-less, unique.

A body that once was,

is alive

Golden

Golden brown skin, glistening with health and adventure.

A consequence of fun, an existence in the sunshine.

Sudden shock, a redirected lifestyle.

The warm sun, replaced with surgery lights and isolation.

Pale white skin, glowing with illness and despair.

A consequence of pain, an existence in the darkness.

Soul Mate

My reflection exposed a bald, broken soul,

an image of weakness and self-defeat.

He looked at me,

With adoration in his eyes,

With an embrace from his heart,

He exposed my beauty.

an image of pure love and friendship.

My soul mate.

I Believe

I believe in life,

a world full of wonder

The sunshine and the waterfalls

Lightning with the thunder.

I see the world so differently

After facing pure fear,

The magic that surrounds us,

To happiness I will steer.

To feel the sun upon my skin,

Won't hide away inside.

For nature helps to heal me,

Makes pain and stress subside.

The colours of a sunset,

From orange, purple, blue.

The warmth that slowly drifts away,

To end the whole day through.

All the things I love the most

That keep the sad at bay.

The following are the best of all,

That ground me when I stray.

To throw a shell amongst the waves,

To build the sand up high.

Sunburnt cheeks and laughter,

Summer times fly by.

Winter comes, the river roars,

Cold splashing at my toes.

Stones are skimmed across the top,

Then tumble as it flows.

The rain that falls so heavily

when days have been so dry.

Smells of freshness fill the air,

Clouds of grey float by.

I once took these for granted

And now these days I see.

Nature is my grounding place,

My favourite place to be.

Time

I need time.

Time to heal,

Time to strengthen,

Time to love.

To watch my children grow.

Time is everything.

Without it, I have nothing.

I need time

To grow old.

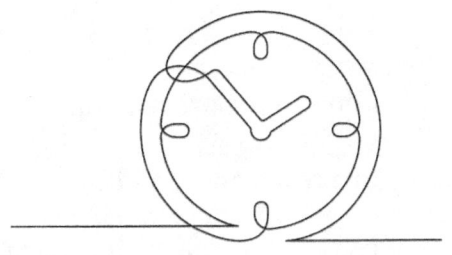

Dream

We always dream, what life could be,

The things that make it great.

The Aussie dream, big cozy house,

Here in the western state.

Since times got tough, saw cancer through.

We realized more than ever.

Our Aussie dream has changed for now,

It's really now or never.

Our health and kids are thriving now,

Money's not our main concern,

We've learned through this, that time is gold

Doesn't matter what you earn.

I do still dream of living,

In a mansion on a hill.

For now, though, just to be alive

I'd give up every bill.

BRCA 1

Genetics once unknown to me,

Have really played a role.

My life got flipped upside down,

The life genetics stole.

Mutation in my makeup,

Passed down through generations.

BRCA 1 was diagnosed

And stopped all celebrations.

The cause of my disease was known,

At least I had an answer,

My breasts and both my ovaries

Removed to combat cancer.

My cancer's gone and now I face,

The second phase of treatment.

Ovaries out, menopause

I'll do it for completement.

I'm 32 and god this sucks,

I wonder why it chose me.

BRCA 1 has played a role,

And genetics was the key.

Unlucky

A drink or two to celebrate,

the end light could be seen.

The needles and the pain had stopped,

The happiest I had been.

My friends and I would laugh and joke,

I showed them both my scars.

We ordered us a ride share,

Why'd we get inside that car?

A moment that changed all of us,

A collision from the side.

We threw ourselves to safety

A minute left of our ride.

Passersby came flocking,

They saw it all unfold.

Strangers came from left and right

Our cold hands they would hold.

It rained until St John appeared

They held umbrellas high,

The angels in the ambulance,

They kept us calm and dry.

The three of us got taken,

To hospitals a far,

A long night lying, wondering,

Why'd we get inside that car.

The injuries sustained that night,

We're not what I had needed,

I was on track, recovering

Felt like I'd been stampeded.

More surgery took place from there,

To fix up all the damage.

Our health care system once again,

Stepped up and helped me manage.

Anxiety

Anxiety, my stomach flips,

My hands will sometimes shake.

The fear of something happening,

The thoughts that make me wake.

I have to live, my new life,

Like not many people do,

I have to always be alert,

To have a different view.

The thoughts of bad things coming,

Will never leave my mind.

I have to try to do my best

To leave it all behind.

I wish that I could go back,

To the days of carefree life.

But anxiety and my healthcare

Play havoc as a wife.

My family once again are strong,

They know that I still need them.

My husband stands right by me,

My anxiety we'll condemn.

Exit Door

Some days are hard, a brick wall of difficulties.

Search for an exit, and overcome the unthinkable

Search for a door, hidden amongst your troubles

A warm welcome on the other side.

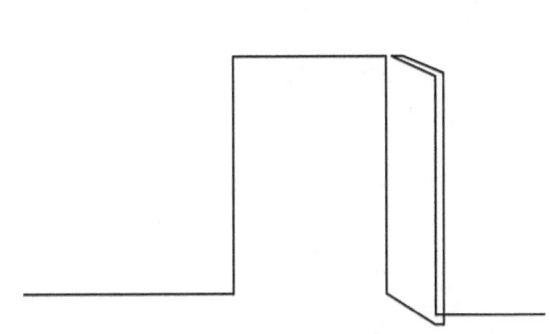

Preach

The amount of women around the world,

Diagnosed with this disease.

We'll come together and fight back hard,

Can I ask you something, please?

Be sure to check your body,

Any changes tell your doctor.

The lump she found, a silly thought,

A thought that they had mocked her.

Turns out life is precious,

Your life is in your hands,

The doctor helps those silly thoughts,

The doctor understands.

In my case I was lucky,

We caught it thanks to me.

My intuition helped myself

Now I need to plea.

Live for Them

Be sure to check your body,

You won't ever have regrets,

I hope it all turns out ok,

Get rid of all the threats.

Good luck to all those women,

Facing hell, no end in sight.

You've got this, don't give up just yet.

Keep fighting this tough fight.

End

You are strong, whatever the hurdle –
jump it with a smile.

Deborah Fullwood
Wife, Mother and Cancer Warrior

www.ingramcontent.com/pod-product-compliance
Lightning Source LLC
Chambersburg PA
CBHW020921140626
46545CB00015B/1159